Hither and Yon

Stories and Illustrations

from my Travels

by

Donette Dunaway Lee

*To Diane —
Thank you so much
for your valuable help
with this project —
You are a dear friend.
Donette*

Hiram, Georgia
2014

Hither and Yon
Stories and Illustrations from My Travels
by
Donette Dunaway Lee

ISBN-13: 978-1500654771
ISBN-10: 1500654779

Available from www.amazon.com, www.createspace.com, and www.donettetravels.com

Front Cover - Sketch from apartment window in Murlo, Italy, overlooking village square

Back Cover - Sketch outside our apartment in Il Casa Grande agritourismo in Umbria, Italy

Dedication

To all the many people with whom I have traveled, both old friends and new. Some are now just names in my sketchbooks, but some have been a part of my life for many years.

To Mother and Daddy, who opened my eyes to the pleasures of exploring.

To Sue Spitchley, who was as enthusiastic about travel as I and was always willing to be our driver, while letting me to plan the trips.

To the W Bunch, who have made every effort to travel to a new spot each year, just in order to keep the flame of friendship alive and well.

To Larry and Sue, Steve and Trish, who encourage my travel and sometimes join me on the road.

And to my daughters who take delight in every new adventure that comes my way. I wish for them many happy travels in the years to come. I hope I have convinced them of its value to a life well lived.

Contents

Chapter	Title	Page

Foreword

Last year I wrote a little memoir to give to my family, sharing memories and stories from my past that I had never collected in one place before. I expected that to be the only book I would ever write.

But sometimes inspiration dawns at odd times, as it did one day when I was sitting at brunch with friends in the Greenbrooke Community. While telling them tales of the several times I have lost belongings or gotten lost myself while traveling, it occurred to me that it might be a good thing to gather my travel stories in one volume.

My multiple watercolor journals, which my daughters have "claimed" for their inheritance, will provide the basis for this collection. Hopefully, they will be interesting to others as well.

Donette
October, 2014

A Tourist's Prayer
(anonymous)

Heavenly Father, look down on your humble tourists who travel this earth mailing postcards, walking around in drip-dry underwear, carrying arms full of souvenirs.

We beseech you that our plane be on time, that we receive our very own baggage at each stop, that our over-weight baggage go unnoticed, and the customs officials are always understanding.

Lead us to good inexpensive restaurants where the wine is included in the price of the meal and the coffee is not too strong to drink.

Give us the strength to visit museums and cathedrals but if we skip historic monuments to take a nap after lunch, have mercy on us for our flesh is weak.

Protect our wives from bargains they don't need and cannot afford, lead them not into temptation for they know not what they do.

Save our husbands from looking at foreign women and comparing them to us. Save them from making fools of themselves in hotels and on ships and please do not forgive them their trespasses for they know exactly what they do.

And when our voyage is over and we return to our loved ones, grant us the favor of finding someone who will look at our photos and listen to our stories. We ask this on behalf of all airlines, hotels and ships at sea and all wonderful, understanding natives who took the time to help.

Amen

Chapter 1
A Lifelong Love

"It is good to have an end to journey toward, but it is the journey that matters in the end."
— *Ernest Hemingway*

Taking trips, seeing new places, having different adventures was ingrained in me from an early age. Because my daddy loved to tell stories about historical events, he would make things come alive for me whenever we went somewhere as a family. Visiting the Civil War battlefield at Vicksburg is an early memory of mine. We climbed to the top of the bluff overlooking the Mississippi River while Daddy explained how, for a while, the Confederate forces withstood the onslaught from the Union army.

Our family could not afford long, elaborate vacations but we would take trips to Panama City to enjoy the beach and swimming in the Gulf of Mexico. Often we would join the Wengers, Aunt Suzette, Uncle Don, Peggy and Larraine, who drove down from Montgomery, Alabama. The adults loved to play bridge, and because no one worried about children outside the cabin alone, they would "banish" us to the beach to allow them a peaceful game of cards. That's where we met the college guys from North Carolina who invited Peggy and me to a movie. (Funny how minor details stick in your mind--my new friend was named Sam Turnipseed!) In 1952 no one assumed that this might have been dangerous. We had a great time.

I loved visiting with my Wenger cousins who lived in the big city of Montgomery. We would spend a month together each summer, alternating between Hollandale and Montgomery. It was time to take Peggy home one year when we were young teenagers, and true to Daddy's pattern, he told Mother he wanted to leave early and drive as far as possible that night. We made it to Tuscaloosa when my parents decided we would stop for the night, but the only place we could find a room was in the old Tuscaloosa Hotel at the top of the hill approaching downtown. All night long as huge trucks approached the hill, they switched to second gear to grind and growl their way up the steep incline. (There were no interstates in the early 50's.)

But the breaking point came when a man with a booming voice, perched on a straight chair down on the front sidewalk, began to "pontificate" to a companion after we turned out our lights to sleep. In an un-air conditioned building, in our third floor room, we slept with the windows open, thus we could hear every word. Peggy and I tried calling out "please be quiet," but when that didn't work, we decided to get his attention by dripping a little water on his head. But the glass slipped and the entire contents spilled, drenching the man and the sidewalk. We ran next door to tell Daddy what had happened and about that time, the phone rang. Of course the manager wanted to inform my parents about the misbehavior of their children. I was never more happy with my daddy than when I heard him inform the manager that it was totally unacceptable for the hotel to allow someone to make so much noise that it kept the guests from sleeping. We slept fine the rest of the night.

A visit to New Orleans coincided with my fifteenth birthday. While there we saw the new movie *Showboat* and my birthday present was the album from the movie with Ann Blythe and Howard Keel. One of our regular places to visit was Natchez, Mississippi, because my mother's siblings (Pyrons and Wengers) all lived there. All four families were in the furniture business, competitors, but still family. We attended the Pilgrimage of antebellum homes, visiting such beautiful mansions as Rosalie, Stanton Hall and Longwood. Daddy's love of history was infectious as he shared details about what we were seeing.

We also went to sporting events, such as state high school basketball tournaments in Jackson or college football games. With Daddy behind the wheel, I was given the map so that I could "navigate." I loved studying maps, reading the interesting names along the way, matching them with the signs we approached on the highway. Sometimes we ran into problems on our journeys, like the night we were driving back to Hollandale from Natchez when a deer jumped in front of our Pontiac. It was pitch dark, the car was not drivable, and we were just north of Port Gibson, ninety miles from home. A good Samaritan stopped to see if he could help. When Daddy explained our plight, this kind man took a chain from his trunk, attached it to our front bumper, and towed us to our house. Then he refused to accept any pay for his kindness.

It the 1970's, their three children educated and on their own, my parents were able to take extended trips. They enjoyed traveling with Mother's brothers and sister and spouses, often in a motorhome for two to three weeks across many states.

But many of their trips, particularly abroad, were with Paul and Margaret Watson, friends from their years together in high school. Mother faithfully recorded their adventures in photo albums with detailed captions. She also kept a notebook with her and recorded what they ate, where it was, and how much it cost. We would laugh at all the minutiae and attribute it to one of Mother's quirks, little realizing that many years later those little notes would prove very interesting. And of course little did I know that the minutiae in my own notebook/journals would be so valuable to me.

Daddy often told me that he wanted to go back to Ireland and take me with him; that seemed to be a place that captured his heart. The year that my daughter Marietta graduated from high school he urged me to plan a trip for us, but I convinced him that going to Washington, D.C. would be more "doable" than a trip abroad. The four of us had a very good trip, even though thinking back, I probably crammed too much into a short time for parents in their 70's. Now in my 70's I can understand how all the hurrying and walking must have been exhausting for them. But they were troopers, never complaining, and always eager to experience new sights.

Some of our favorite "Deloris stories" even now are those we heard when they returned from a trip because her brothers teased her unmercifully; she was very naive. They never let her forget hitting the jackpot at the nickel slots in Las Vegas, good Baptist lady that she was. After gathering all her nickels in her purse, they insisted that she could not return to Hollandale with that gambling money, so she was responsible for buying their ice cream for the rest of the trip.

A story I heard as a child before I even understood its significance was from their going out on the town in New Orleans. The nightspot they chose was the My-O-My Club. Mother was enthralled with the beautiful showgirls who danced and entertained them. She kept talking about them after they headed to the hotel, when the men decided to clue her in: the entertainers were drag queens. Mortified to have been admiring cross-dressing men, she had a hard time living that down.

5

These stories were told and retold when our extended family would gather. I knew that some day I wanted to travel to interesting places and see unusual things. But my opportunity didn't arrive until after I retired at the end of 1994. Until that time I was busy with two daughters, a full time career with the telephone company, and the responsibility of two college educations. But I didn't forget the dream. In 1995, while working at the Jackson, Mississippi, exhibition from the Palaces of St. Petersburg, I was able to travel to Russia with the advance publicity tour for journalists previewing the exquisite artwork. This was my first passport and my first trip abroad; I vowed that it would not be my last.

But before I tell stories from some of my lengthy trips away from home, I want to start with a spur-of-the-minute, unplanned trip that showed me how valuable a role traveling could play in my life. It is a very personal story and yet it holds a significant spot in the travelogue of my life.

6

Chapter 2
When Travel Becomes Therapy

"Learning to trust the healing properties of the beauty that surrounds me has become a spiritual discipline in my life. It takes practice, yet when I am faithful to the practice, I find it increasingly medicinal."

—*Macrina Wiederkehr*

When we plan a trip we may have any number of reasons for setting out—adventure, relaxation, fun or change of scenery. But there are times when travel can provide therapy and healing.

Such was my trip with the handbell choir from Mississippi Southern, which had been paid in advance for the late spring of 2000. In April I learned that I had to have a major operation but that day in the doctor's office my concern was focused more on whether I could recuperate in time to take the trip than on having to undergo surgery at all. I did recover quickly and the marvelous journey across Europe was like the best medicine. I do not remember having any anxiety about my health, then or anytime since.

There was one excursion in 1996 that was literally for my mental health. I had suffered several losses over the course of about two years and realized that I needed to address what effect this was having on my well-being. The lingering sadness over the loss of my mother in 1994 was with me constantly. At the end of that same year I had retired from my career with the telephone company.

Although this event was a happy one, coming to terms with the drastic change in lifestyle required serious psychological effort. After that retirement I had worked for the Mississippi Commission for International Cultural Exchange to prepare for the exhibit from the Palaces of St. Petersburg. But on opening day, the executive director dismissed me, alleging that the board had drastically cut the budget. (The fact that he and I could not see eye to eye was not mentioned.) This blow (mostly to my ego) just added to my growing depression. Furthermore, my dad's health was rapidly deteriorating in the wake of losing his lifelong companion.

The catalyst that spurred me to action came from a different source. For the past year I had enjoyed a relationship with a man who had been a friend for many years. We enjoyed many of the same interests, mutual friends, even the same church. But when I learned that he was seeing someone else at the same time, I knew that it was time to bring our relationship to a close. Unfortunately, I continued to feel the hurt from that loss; it was painful to hear his voice behind me every week in the church choir. The grief from all of these losses began to escalate and build to an unbearable degree.

One Sunday morning as I listened to our pastor, Roger Paynter, share his plans for an upcoming Sabbatical, I experienced a clear epiphany. I, too, could take a Sabbatical. And so I did. Within a few days, I had packed suitcases and car to start driving northeast. Without any detailed planning (as is my usual habit), I drove to Brooksville, Mississippi, to visit with Sister Clare, the director of The Dwelling Place.

Located in a secluded rural setting, this lovely, quiet retreat center had been a special place for me in the past; it seemed like a good place to start my journey.

Sister Clare—I think of her that way even though she is no longer a nun—welcomed me warmly and suggested that I stay a few days. She offered me lodging in one of the three "hermitages," tiny one room cottages designed for individual quiet space. She also said that she would be available for a counseling session each day if I chose. The library was available for my use and she recommended that I read Joyce Rupp's *Praying Our Goodbyes*. What a perfect book for me at that time! Each chapter in the book deals with some type of loss—death, retirement, divorce, etc. I spent my time reflecting on her words, delving into my feelings, allowing myself to cry; I also wrote page after page in my journal. One of the recommendations that appealed to me was to write letters to the people over whom I was grieving. I could pour out my hurt and regret, my anger and disappointment, knowing that all of these words were between me and God. The book further recommended a ritual to conclude the process, specifically praying and releasing them to God. I found a spot as I walked around the lake where I could bury the scraps of paper in the mud and walk away. It was symbolic, but it was also immensely satisfying.

I don't have as clear memories of the rest of that trip except that I know I was gone for two weeks, still traveling east toward South Carolina. I spent a few days with my sister, then turned north toward the Blue Ridge mountains.

Somewhere in north Georgia

Nothing is more comforting to me than spending time in the high elevations of western North Carolina. Turning back west I traveled to Murfreesboro, Tennessee, to visit awhile with cousins Peggy and Larraine. Enjoying being together since childhood, those memories are fun to recover as we laugh and talk. Since I was in no hurry, I took the leisure route home by way of the Natchez Trace Parkway, where the speed limit is 50 miles per hour. But that lovely road through northeast Mississippi is also very calming and refreshing.

After getting back to my home in Ridgeland, I knew that I was in a much better place than when I left. I had obtained some healing for the hurts, some closure for past regrets. I had also learned that putting distance between me and reminders of the pain could aid my healing; therefore, I decided to "church hop" for a while. I visited a different church every Sunday, various denominations, wherever the Spirit led. At the end of three months I was ready to return to my home church (even though it took a little longer before I rejoined the choir). Traveling alone **can** be therapeutic.

The Lonely Moors of Yorkshire

Chapter 3
Playing While I Worked

"I'm good at working, but I'm very good at playing."
—*Salma Hayek*

During my career with South Central Bell and ultimately BellSouth, I had an opportunity to do a lot of travel. For our district meetings we would go to various cities within our nine state territory such as Nashville, New Orleans, Atlanta and Birmingham. When we were still a part of AT&T there were occasions to travel to New Jersey for training sessions in the AT&T facilities at Morristown. After previously having unfavorable mental images of "Joisey," I remember being impressed with the beauty of that state, because its motto as The Garden State is well deserved.

A couple of my business trips have stuck in my mind. I had the opportunity to take a fascinating training course in South Florida which started with 3 days in Fort Lauderdale studying important writings from the past. We began with Plato's "Republic" and concluded with Martin

Luther King's "Letter from Birmingham Jail." What a stimulating experience that proved to be, not business focused, but enriching and mentally challenging. From there we were transferred to one of the Keys, traveling by boat from Key West. While on the island we spent three days in an outdoor course on the order of Outward Bound.

An interesting phenomenon of that course was the obvious disparity between women and men. Even though we were equals in pay grade and company status, when the various exercises were presented, the men forged into all the leadership roles. Even our ideas were not taken seriously, in spite of the expressed purpose of learning cooperation and teamwork. On one assignment I made a suggestion for a strategy; it was ignored. A few minutes later a man proposed the same approach; it was immediately adopted by the group. When the final debriefing took place at the conclusion, the women began to unload their frustrations in front of the whole group and the men were stunned. The leaders of the exercise were very supportive and pointed out to them that this is a microcosm of their work place. They were admonished to remember these lessons when they returned to their jobs.

Another specific memory is from one of my trips to Birmingham. As we waited in the gate area to board our plane, I noticed dozens of young girls ready to leave for Camp DeSoto in Alabama. Booked into Seat 16A, I was standing close to a girl who was distraught because she could not be seated with her friends. She was offered the only seat left on the plane, <u>which was in first class.</u> I graciously offered to change seats with her, since my assigned seat was in coach next to her best friend. She never missed the luxury of those wide leather seats, but I enjoyed every minute of that flight.

A nice side benefit of all these trips was accumulating frequent flier miles which I could use for personal travel later. At one point there was a rumor that the company would "confiscate" our frequent flier points, since the flights were paid with company funds. There was a hew and cry over this possibility, since we believed (rightly, I think) that we were due the perk in exchange for our personal wear and tear.

Grey, gloomy day out the airport window, waiting to board

Chapter 4
Did I Mention That I Sang at Carnegie Hall?

"Hallelujah!"

Maybe being only one voice out of ninety doesn't exactly make me a star, but the experience was as exciting as if I had had the stage to myself!

It happened like this: No longer having use of company computers after I retired, I immediately purchased my first desktop PC. As with every new gadget I acquire, I spent hours just practicing, playing games, and searching the internet. My internet provider at the time was AOL and one day in mid-1997 I noticed a "click here" button that said, "SING at Carnegie Hall."

Out of curiosity I clicked and read that a chorus was being recruited from across the country. But what got my attention was that the conductor would be none other than John Rutter from England. Our choirs in recent years had sung many of his compositions; his recordings with the Cambridge Singers are among my favorites. Added to that, the chosen work for the performance would be *"Messiah"* by Handel.

This was the perfect combination for me; what did I have to lose by applying? The announced schedule involved being in New York over the Thanksgiving weekend for the concert on Sunday afternoon. I called to tell Sue to go online and retrieve an application form; the deadline was August 31, giving us only a couple of days to make our decision. In 1997 using the internet was much less commonplace than now, but we submitted the forms by email the next day. The second step was to send a vocal recording to Mid America Productions.

Billy Trotter, organist at Northminster, graciously agreed to work with us. The sound system for the church was capable of making cassette tapes and each of us sang a verse of *Amazing Grace* to Billy's accompaniment. I certainly didn't profess to be a soloist, but I convinced myself that they were looking for people who could stay on pitch, had good diction and could project their voices. In any case, within a week both of us had been accepted to sing with ninety other choristers recruited online.

The internet played an even greater role in this project as message boards were set up to allow the participants to get to know each other in advance. We could talk to the others in the chat room, speculating on just what we could anticipate. In a planned group chat in November, Maestro Rutter came on to give last minute instructions to the group while we made notes in our scores. (Today we could have "Skyped" and actually talked to him face to face.)

We flew into New York on Wednesday, enjoying watching the Macy's Thanksgiving Day parade in person. We were booked in the Grand Hyatt hotel at a great location near Grand Central Station. The first rehearsal was scheduled for five p.m. on Thursday afternoon at a nearby rehearsal hall. On the stroke of 5:00 Rutter entered to our applause, nodding his acknowledgement. Mounting the podium he announced the page number, gave a downbeat and we were off—no preliminaries or warm up.

Most of the people had good choral background and were proficient in singing large works of music. Here and there we learned that some had never sung *"Messiah,"* which surprised me. But in my alto section I sat by a New Yorker who sang regularly in the choir at the Cathedral of St. John the Divine in New York. Her diction was flawless. Rutter's demeanor was very low key but his methods were exacting. To achieve a harmonious blend from so many disparate voices was a credit to his genius.

We rehearsed on Friday and Saturday, reporting early to Carnegie Hall on Sunday for a final run through. Four professional soloists and the chorus were accompanied by the Brooklyn Symphony Orchestra. The wait until performance time was rather long, but a reporter from the New York Times was making the rounds interviewing various members of the chorus.

When the curtain rose at three p.m. I was surprised to see that every seat in the house was filled. The audience was enthusiastically appreciative, standing for a long ovation at the conclusion. And in the Monday edition of the New York Times, there was a picture of the group with a long article about this "first-of-its kind" concert.

Chapter 5
The Story Behind the Sketchbooks

"When we open ourselves to creativity, we open ourselves to the Creator's creativity within us and our lives."
— Julia Cameron

To explain how I began combining my love for traveling with another of my post-retirement loves, painting, I need to discuss the origin of my sketchbooks. They are the source for many of the stories in this book.

Despite having kept journals for several years, even adding little colored pencil sketches amid the writing, it had never occurred to me that my newly found watercolor hobby could be incorporated into these notebooks. That is, until I met Maggie Hoybach.

Having begun to take art lessons in 1996, I was eager to find good workshops to attend. In the spring of 2001, during a lengthy stay at our condo in Highlands, North Carolina, I learned of a weeklong watercolor workshop at the High Hampton Inn in Cashiers, ten miles away. Without knowing anything other than the instructor was from Charleston, South Carolina, Sue Spitchley and I signed up for her course. This literally set me on a totally new path, not only with my artwork, but also for my future travel. Because Maggie had a passion for watercolor journaling, she described her technique throughout the week. The turning point for me came when she announced that she would be taking a group to Provence, France, the next September to paint in the Luberon Valley.

I knew immediately that this was a trip I had to make. On August 29, 2001, Sue and I, along with our friend, Phyllis Parker, and our Jackson art teacher, Diane Norman, flew to Marseille by way of Paris. Even though our flight from Atlanta was smooth, we landed at Charles de Gaulle airport at 6:30 a.m., only forty-five minutes before our connecting flight to Marseille. There were at least 200 people at passport control, causing us to miss our flight and wait for four hours in the airport. Finally arriving in the south of France, we were met by Maggie and her husband Peter at 2:00 p.m., only to learn that Sue's luggage was not aboard the plane. (It arrived the next day.)

After driving north for an hour and a half to the village of Gordes, then finally making it to our hotel, *Mas de la Senancole*, we were ready to sit by the pool, drink wine and view Maggie's sketchbooks. Our instruction began immediately. She explained to us that we would be expected to take our sketchbooks with us **everywhere**, making sketches, notes, observations, collecting tickets, labels and postcards in addition to pages of actual watercolors from our various locations. The first thing to put in the book was a blank calendar for the dates of the trip; there we could jot down quick notes of where we were that day, because the names of all the places would become jumbled in our minds.

A van would pick us up each morning to take us to a different village where Maggie would give a demo to illustrate various watercolor techniques. She pointed out that the sidewalk cafes were ideal for doing our sketches. All we needed to do was order a pot of tea and the wait staff would let us stay outside all afternoon to paint to our hearts' content. We also carried small collapsible stools that allowed us to perch in any convenient spot to get the right view for our sketches.

Maggie could communicate with the local people just slightly, but it was enough to help us get by. She encouraged us to keep a list of French words and phrases so that we could make ourselves understood in villages where there were few English speakers. My list in the back of the sketchbook was valuable in restaurants when I tried to interpret the menu. But being able to ask for *d'eau chaud* (hot water) was essential when I was served black coffee that was stronger than double espresso. All of Maggie's little tips have given me a foundation, not only for my artwork, but also for every trip that I have taken since then.

Another trick that Maggie showed us was how to peel off the beautiful labels from the wine bottles at our dinner meals. We would take the bottles back to the hotel, soak a

hand towel in water, wrap the wine bottle and leave it overnight. The next day the label could be gently removed and flattened to dry. Later these labels formed beautiful collages in the sketchbooks, reminding us of the variety of wines served during our trip.

She insisted that we learn to make quick sketches just to capture a moment. As we set out for the beautiful hilltop town of Roussillon, glowing from the red clay of its buildings and the cliffs on which it sits, Maggie had our driver stop at an overlook to gaze across the vineyards at the scene. She instructed us to sketch it quickly, giving us only ninety seconds to capture the image. Later I was able to expand that image into a two-page watercolor.

Lundi Matin 8 Septembre
Before entering Roussillon, we parked at a overlook
to sketch the city

From Maggie I learned to really *see* what was in front of me. Until then it had not occurred to me that I should draw the designs from the tablecloth while waiting to be served dinner.

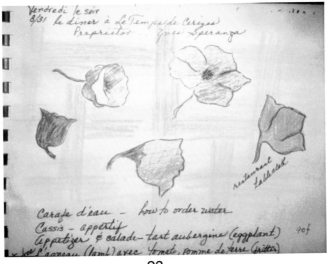

Vendredi le soir
8/31 le diner à Le Temps de Cerises
Proprietor: Yves Speranza

restaurant
tablecloth

Carafe d'eau — how to order water
Cassis - apperitif
Appetizer & salade — tart aubergine (eggplant)   90f
L'agneau (lamb) avec tomate, pomme de terre (fritter)

If I had not sketched the unusual shapes of the ice cream dishes served on the hotel terrace, I would no longer remember the delicious *citron et menthe chocolat* that was so refreshing on a hot afternoon.

And how fabulous it is to have images of Cezanne's studio, where we were forbidden to take our cameras. Many times I have been reminded of the door that was two stories tall and two feet wide which had been built to transport his enormous canvases out of the studio.

When Maggie told us to carry the sketchbooks everywhere we went, I took her seriously. Every evening in the hotel I would write about our activities that day and put final touches on my artwork. My diligence paid off because on the last day Maggie critiqued our work, awarding me the prize for most complete sketchbook. I will be forever grateful to Maggie for giving me such a basic understanding of travel journals and helping me to see the endless possibilities that they afford. All these many years later I can return to those experiences with much more passion than I ever could with a photograph album. I now have sketchbooks from every trip I have taken.

Sunflowers from a French garden, sketched as we visited on the terrace

The date we arrived home is indelibly printed in my mind: September 10, 2001. Returning to Atlanta, Sue and I spent the night at Marietta's apartment where we were having a cup of coffee while watching the "Today Show" on Tuesday morning, September 11. As events of that awful day unfolded I realized that one day later we would have been stranded in the airport in Marseille.

Chapter 6
Best Friends Forever

"Women have rarely known primacy in temples or churches, and so we continue to find it at <u>other</u> altars, with our sisters, who have <u>never</u> lacked for words, only voices and volume. "

—Martha Manning

Most everyone would agree with me that life long friends are gifts to be treasured. However, it never occurred to me that getting to know a group of girls during my college days at MSCW would stretch out over the next sixty years and provide an annual gathering in far flung locations around the South. I met Ellen Young on High School Weekend in 1953; we signed up for a room and we were roommates for four years. Sixty-one years later, we are still roommates when we travel with The W Bunch.

We belonged to the Jester Social Club, from the classes of 1956, 1957 and 1958; as time passed, we dubbed ourselves The W Bunch. After graduation we scattered to begin careers or marriage, some with young families already. But we tried to reconnect periodically, often at Christmastime in Jackson when we returned to Mississippi for the holidays. Those early meetings were usually dinner at a local restaurant; some of us included our husbands.

But as our children grew older and we had a bit more freedom, we could manage a weekend away from home. The earliest of these outings was near Louisville, Mississippi, at Lake Tiak O'Khata where we could rent cabins and eat in their dining hall. Sylvia (Duckie) Clark lived in Louisville

and made the arrangements for us. At that time she was co-owner of a dress shop named "Mirror Mirror." The highlight of the weekend was shopping with our own personal consultant, who graciously granted us a 20% discount on purchases.

In the intervening years we have traveled several times to Edisto Beach, South Carolina, at Betty Lewis' invitation; once we visited in Geri Ingram's home at Sautee, Georgia; Sally McReynolds entertained us at least twice in Shelbyville, Tennessee; Nan Long gave us access to vacation homes of her children in Port St. Joe, Florida and Pickwick Lake, Mississippi; and Duckie opened her condo in Orange Beach, Alabama, on several occasions.

Beach trips provided great subject matter for sketching

Other trips have been planned for hotels, condos, beach houses and conference centers in fun places like Black Mountain, Highlands, and Blowing Rock, North Carolina; Jekyll Island, and Callaway Gardens, Georgia; Ft. Morgan, Alabama; Gray Center and Plymouth Bluff in Mississippi.

We have embraced new adventures: riding on Sally's Sea Doo at Tims Ford Lake, hiking to Sunset Rock to overlook Highlands, fishing at Gray Center and Pickwick Lake, and hiking to Anna Ruby Falls in north Georgia. And we have seen the sights: the Majesty of Spain exhibit and the Museum of Natural Science in Jackson; buggy riding in Charleston, South Carolina; feeling the wind at the top of Blowing Rock, North Carolina; taking a historical walking tour of Beaufort, South Carolina; and of course, shopping in at least seven different states.

Our most recent trip in 2014 gave us a chance to return to Homecoming at the W as well as spend a day at Mississippi State enjoying the annual Ragtime and Blues Festival and visit Tex and Carolyn's lovely condo, while staying at Plymouth Bluff Conference Center. With no activities planned for Sunday morning, we had a memorial worship service to honor the first loss of a member of our group. In February our sweet precious Jo Nell Hales died quietly in her sleep in Birmingham. Ten of us were able to attend her funeral and it seemed appropriate for us to honor her again privately when we gathered in March.

We sang, read Scripture, and prayed; then Sally spoke for a few minutes about "The Ties That Bind," a reflection in memory of Jo Nell and in honor of the strong bonds that exist within this group. Quoting from Sally's remarks that day:

Jo Nell Thomas Hales 1935 - 2014

"To begin with, MSCW was the tie that brought us together. Through activities in smaller groups like Jesters, college singers, BSU or Wesley, Meh Lady, Spectator, Theater Guild and Student Government, we built friendships and developed common interests. But what ties have kept us together all these 60 years? We have not all lived in the same communities. Some of us married while others did not. We pursued different careers, joined different organizations and churches, and supported different charities. I suggest to you that it might be those differences that tie us together. God gave us different talents and we have used those talents to knit a group of kindred minds together in Christian love.

"Those in our group who are musically talented have led us in memorable experiences. We remember singing in the Church in the Wildwood, the chapel in Callaway Gardens with its magnificent stained glass window and melodious organ music, the Grand Ole Opry in Nashville, the piano and sing-a-long at Port St. Joe, another sing-a-long at the chapel in The Cove in North Carolina with Janet at the piano, and at the Gray Center in Canton where we had our own little church to sing and worship. We even sang camp songs at Tims Ford Lake in Tennessee. Jo Nell was inspired by the breakfast music at Highlands and found "Scottish Tranquility" on a tape which she copied for each of us. And most recently we attended the Ragtime Festival at Mississippi State.

"Some of us are talented and educated in the field of home economies. Think of the delicious food our talented cooks have prepared and served so elegantly. Bacon wrapped green beans by Jo Nell comes to mind. That bowl of boiled shrimp and platter of corn-on-the-cob with new potatoes served by Beverly and Duckie at Edisto was a low country delight. Of course we all love Beckly's pimento cheese. Desserts and goodies too numerous to mention (often provided by Douglas Ann) added flare to our meals. The creative members saw to it that the tables were set with appropriate and available decor, i.e. magnolia blossoms at Jekyll Island..."

The wide ranging life experiences within this group of sixteen women have enriched all of us. Bev Jones was dedicated to her work with Girl Scouts; when we had a few hours in Savannah, it was important to her to tour the homeplace of the founder, Juliette Lowe.

Becky has donated untold hours to Mustard Seed, a daycare facility for developmentally challenged adults. She arranged a tour for us through their ceramic workshop and we were enchanted as they eagerly showed us their artwork. Later in the gift shop we

bought lots of colorful items to remind us of a unique experience. I treasure my little teapot.

On one of our trips to Edisto, Betty arranged a walking tour of nearby Beaufort, South Carolina, where learning about the history of the low country was entertaining and educational. Our guide (a former actor) loved to talk, and during his rambling discourse there was

Tabernacle
Baptist
Church
founded 1840

plenty of time to sketch this old church, Tabernacle Baptist, founded in 1840 and given to the slaves by the Union army after they invaded South Carolina.

While traveling in North Carolina in 2007 we wanted to see the Grove Park Inn in Asheville. But as we arrived, so did a thunderstorm. Racing inside out of the rain, we strolled and looked, then

decided to take a group picture standing in front of the enormous fireplace in their lobby. That was when the electricity went out. Beverly, who had parked her van **underground**, said "I better go get the van; you round up the girls." We waited at the front door quite a while before she drove up, tears in her eyes from laughing, to recount her adventure: Without electricity or elevators, she had to walk down to the sixth level, but there was no entrance. She stopped a maid who said, "No English." She walked down more stairs to the fourth floor, where she was told to go back up to sixth and look for a tiny car sign over the door to "Sammons Garage." Finally inside, in total darkness, she had to flick the remote control for the car lights in order to locate the van.

Occasionally we wonder how long we will be able to continue our trips, but we all know that they have a high priority on everyone's calendar. Sally ended her remarks that Sunday in March 2014 by saying, "After the benediction I invite you to share some of your memories of Jo Nell." And we did...surprisingly, they were not sorrowful, rather they were mostly joyful...and yes, even funny. We all have special memories of Jo Nell and also of Nan, who succumbed a few months later to her lingering illness. We cherish each and every member of our group. The recent coining of "BFF" has almost become trite, but in some cases, "best friends forever" is actually true.

Edisto Island

Tiak O'Khata 1987

Callaway Gardens 1998

Church in the Wildwood
Highlands, North Carolina 1993

At the W in 2014

Chapter 7
Beaches in July

"We do not quit playing because we grow old; we grow old because we quit playing."
— *George Bernard Shaw*

In the summer of 2008 all twenty-nine members of the Dunaway family, children and grandchildren of W.A. and Deloris, gathered at Lake Louisa near Clermont, Florida, for a long weekend reunion. We had four houses along the waterfront on either side of Larry and Sue's lake house. It was an ideal setup, allowing the children complete freedom to scamper from one house to the other, while adults rocked on the screened porches.

Because of severe drought the water level was very, very low. Larry had to drag his boat across sand to get it

launched. But because the water along the shore was only one foot deep, the children could safely play while adults visited in beach chairs.

Each day one of the family groups hosted the evening meal and afterward we played "intergenerational" games such as "Catch Phrase." Playing games with adults in the family has always been a favorite memory of my daughters and we loved sharing that experience with the next generation.

Because my grandson Zach turned five on July 20 we invited everyone to his birthday party on Saturday afternoon, We had a piñata, balloons, and pin-the-tail-on-the-donkey. It was such a big hit that Zach requested another party at the lake the next year.

One of the most talented members of our family is Larry and Sue's grandson, Liam, who was seventeen at the time of the reunion. With his ever-present camera, he documented the entire event, even taking family group portraits, organizing everyone and managing it all in twenty minutes. He was able to set up time delay to get in the center of the picture just in front of his parents, Beth and Will.

Lake Louisa Pier

This trip to Florida dovetailed nicely with the Jekyll Island Wretreat that was in progress when I arrived on Sunday. [The spelling of Wretreat is not accidental, as this group of MUW alums had been labeled "renegades" by the administration of our university. Turning it to our advantage by adding the W, we became the Wrens, and this group of loyal dissenters has continued to bond in the years since the debacle which began when our alumni association was disaffiliated from the university. Happily, since new brooms sweep clean, the current administration has seen the value of having a united alumni body and we are once again back in favor at our beloved alma mater.] But I digress.

The idea began to circulate on our listserve that we could congregate on the coast of Georgia to get to know each other better, and in some cases, to meet for the first time. That was also the week of my birthday and the highlight for me was the surprise party with a large basket of Creative Memories scrapbooking supplies. I was able to preserve my memories from the summer in the scrapbooks that I received.

During our week together I had lots of time to sketch; the location is perfect for that pastime. Here are a few of the scenes that I captured:

Three interesting palmetto trees behind Jekyll Island Club

The gargoyles on Faith Chapel fascinated me

St. Simon's Lighthouse

On a day trip to St. Simon's Island, I recorded this view

I sat in the crook of a low-hanging limb while I painted.

Clump of wax myrtles atop dunes near King Street

The weather at the beach was perfect for painting on the morning of my seventy-third birthday.

Chapter 8
Flowers with Jackie

"Earth's crammed with heaven, and every common bush afire with God: But only he who sees takes off his shoes.
— *Elizabeth Barrett Browning*

One of my first friends in Georgia was Jackie Gibson. At the time we met she was still single (Rich entered the picture a year or so later) and we would go on little day

trips, usually at her instigation. Jackie is a gardener and, while I am not, she knew that I was always willing to go with her to visit lovely places.

She invited me to attend the Atlanta Garden Show, a tour of personal gardens mostly in the Decatur area. We enjoyed the day, but it was a lot of driving and walking to see gardens that were less than spectacular.

She was a member of the Atlanta Botanical Gardens and on another occasion she invited me as her guest to tour their lovely grounds. Rich assured me I would be doing him a favor to accompany her (thereby freeing him to do his own thing). Never having been to this venue I enjoyed it thoroughly with Jackie as my expert guide to tell me all about the various varieties of flowers and plants.

One spring a friend from Black Mountain, North Carolina, came to visit on the weekend of our annual church gala, St. Julian's Idol. Seated next to Jackie, my friend Geri began to describe a festive weekend "Art in Bloom" held every June in Black Mountain. Jackie immediately said "I want to go; Donette, let's do it." And so we did. Geri arranged for us to stay in the guest apartment at their retirement community. Our weekend included garden tours, a luncheon and a delightful theater production. My favorite event was the art show in which each painting was interpreted with a floral design by one of the local members. At a tea party/fashion show we enjoyed "delectables" and tea served from handmade pottery tea pots.

After tea was served we were treated to a style show of "wearable art." Every garment was made from natural fibers, handwoven, knitted, silk screened by local fiber artists. One unique item was a raincoat made from recycled billboard posters. Jackie found an elegant patchwork coat, full length and woven from variegated turquoise yarn. She knew that Rich would love for her to buy this as an early Christmas present.

It was a memorable weekend and the time when I began to realize that my friend Jackie was totally spontaneous. I loved being included in her adventures.

Cashiers, NC Enjoying the dahlias

Having told Jackie and Rich about Highlands, North Carolina, from my years with a summer home there, they had also grown to love that area. One day Jackie called to say, "How would you like to go with me tomorrow to look at dahlias?" "Sure," I said. "Where are we going?" She said "Cashiers" (in North Carolina). I was surprised that she wanted to make such a trip in one day; nevertheless, I agreed to go. We stopped in Highlands for lunch in the

47

courtyard at the Old Edwards Inn, then drove the next ten miles to see the dahlias that grow in abundance at a nursery right on the main highway. While she inspected every variety of dahlia to determine which would be appropriate for her garden, I sat on the porch and sketched the flowers from that shady spot.

She has certainly inspired me to learn and experiment more with flowers than I had done in the past. Although she and Rich moved to Indiana last year, when they came back for her son's wedding in May this year, my opportunity to see them came in the form of an invitation to visit a botanical garden. We drove to Ballground, Georgia, and then ten more miles through the countryside to Gibbs Gardens, an exquisitely landscaped private garden developed over the last thirty years by Jim Gibbs. From the website, the description of the gardens captures the essence of what we saw:

> In northeast Cherokee County, Georgia, capturing a view of the north Georgia mountains, the gardens are composed of 16 gardens, including a Japanese Garden, a Waterlily Garden and the Manor House Garden. Flowing through the middle of the valley is a beautiful stream intersected by hundreds of springs. The springs are surrounded by millions of naturalized ferns. Native azaleas, dogwoods and mountain laurels are scattered throughout. Gibbs designed 24 ponds, 32 bridge crossings and 19 waterfalls. The numerous garden rooms are planted with hundreds of varieties of plants and flowers. The entire property is 292

acres, of which 220 make up the house and gardens. It is
one of the largest residential estate gardens in the nation.

The elegance and beauty of this place was truly memorable. I would have probably never heard of it or had a chance to see it, if not for my flower friend, Jackie and her charming husband, Rich. They have enhanced my love of beauty.

Chapter 9
Traveling for Spiritual Enrichment

"We reach for God in many ways. Through our sculptures and our scriptures. Through our pictures and our prayers. Through our writing and our worship. And through them He reaches for us." — Ken Gire

Even though my original intent to pursue a vocation in ministry did not result in a full-time career, I nevertheless have had a strong need for deepening my relationship with God. Over the years I have taken many trips to places where I could find enlightenment, nourishment, solitude, and comfort. Probably my very favorite is Laity Lodge in the Texas Hill Country. But a weeklong **silent** retreat, led by a favorite writer, Macrina Wiedekehr, at St. Scholastica Monastery in Ft. Smith, Arkansas, was an unforgettable experience. The Dwelling Place in Brooksville, Mississippi, Montreat Assembly (Presbyterian) in Black Mountain, North Carolina, and Kanuga Conference Center (Episcopal) near Henderson, North Carolina, were all educational as well as offering spiritual renewal.

My first experience at Laity Lodge came in 1963 when I was working as Assistant Baptist Student Union Director in Houston, Texas. The BSU was taking a bus to the winter Student Week conference. I returned at least three times years later to attend a variety of conferences. The beauty of central Texas, west of San Antonio near the town of Leakey, is beyond my ability to describe. Laity Lodge is an ecumenical Christian retreat center established in 1961 by Howard Butt, heir to the H-E-B grocery store chain. Scholars, theologians, musicians, artists and guests from all walks of life gather there for the purpose of encouraging and renewing the laity—the people of God.

The quality of the guest leaders at the week-long conferences is superb: in the past they hosted Henri Nouwen, Frederic Buechner, Paul Tournier and Madeleine L'Engle. Even those whose names are not as well known are amazing in their capacity for challenging and evoking deep spiritual experiences from within their listeners. One of my never forgotten moments was in the before-breakfast devotional led by Eddie Sears, the Director of Operations at that time. Eddie quoted a tiny poem by Macrina Weiderkehr:

> "Oh God, help me to believe
> the truth about myself,
> no matter how beautiful it might be."

I was overcome with that image and immediately asked Eddie about the quote. He directed me to the lending library to find her book, *Seasons of Your Heart*. Thus began my continuing love of her poetry.

Kanuga has a history of featuring fine speakers and retreat leaders also. I decided to travel there by myself for the Christianity and Literature conference. After registering I received a thick packet in the mail containing all the "pre-reading" that we were expected to complete before arriving. Although I have long since forgotten exactly what we read, I remember how intellectually challenging it was. The literature was not religious, rather completely secular, but our two leaders, Sam Lloyd from Boston and William Barnwell from New Orleans, were able to take the material and evoke the most meaningful discussions from the participants. Since that time I have always been on the lookout for discussion groups that seek to find the divine in the ordinary.

Kanuga Chapel

The food at both of these centers is a constant source of conversation among attendees. Fabulous meals with marvelous variety made it hard to avoid over indulging. Funnily enough, the one thing that stands out in my mind is the buttered toast at Kanuga. It must have been soaked in melted butter and slowly baked until it was crisp and brown through and through. I have never been able to duplicate it, but if you ask anyone who has ever been there, they will remember the toast at breakfast.

At Montreat Presbyterian Assembly I was able to incorporate my art into the spiritual experience. The most appealing thing about Montreat is its setting nestled in the Blue Ridge mountains, with buildings constructed from the native stones of the area. Central to the property is Lake Susan, with the bookstore and gift shop on its banks, and a

Autumn at Lake Susan Montreat

dam creating a waterfall at the bridge. It is a fabulous place to paint *en plain air*, outside in the breathtaking beauty of autumn foliage.

Many people love to vacation at the beach, soaking up the sun. I have always been drawn to the mountains since my first trip to the Ridgecrest Baptist Assembly as a teenager. Although I know that God is all around us no matter where we may be, I also know for a fact that my most intense spiritual experiences have occurred as I contemplated the majesty of God's handiwork in the North Carolina mountains.

While traveling we always look for opportunities to attend church services, choral concerts, Evensong, or other types of worship experiences. One of the most memorable occurred on Sunday morning in Paris, when our group of four decided to take a taxi to Notre Dame, hoping to hear some fine organ music. But when we arrived we could not enter the cathedral because the plaza was filled with chairs for the outdoor Pentecost celebration. Thousands of people were seated in the square, each person carrying a different colored sheer scarf, which we assumed represented continents or nationality or ethnic heritage. We were handed white scarves as we made our way to a seat. The mass was conducted primarily in French, with prayers and Scripture read in French, English, Portuguese and VietNamese. Before the Eucharist they paused to "pass the peace" and the warmth of the people around us was obvious. Then in our program (written in French) I could translate enough to know that we would repeat the Paternoster (Lord's Prayer) **each in his own language**. The mingling of thousands of voices in multiple languages, all repeating the same prayer, was a very powerful Pentecost symbol.

After attending an Episcopal church for a few years I have come to appreciate the elegant service of Evensong, particularly if the music is offered by a fine choir. Realizing that we would be in England where the Anglican church is known for its lovely music, it was a treat to attend Evensong in two of the great cathedrals. Spending one night in York as we traveled north, we attended the service at York Minster, the magnificent edifice that looms above the surrounding city.

York Minster Cathedral

From there we traveled to Durham where we visited the great Durham Cathedral, part of a World Heritage Site and one of Britain's best loved buildings. Evensong begins every day at 5:15; it so happened that during the week we were there, the choir from St. Paul's church in Fayetteville, Arkansas, sang every afternoon. The choir was outstanding and the student organist was fantastic, playing Bach's *Dorian Toccata* as the postlude. We enjoyed chatting with the young Americans in this beautiful setting.

My search for spiritual enrichment invariably has to include great music. And that has always been available no matter where I have been in the world.

View of Durham Cathedral
from the banks of River Wear and Milburngate Bridge

Chapter 10
Do It Yourself vs Group Travel

I've tried both; I can't say which is better.

At one point I was very "anti-group" because I didn't want to be regimented. Believe me, traveling with a group is regimentation. "Have your bags outside your hotel door at 7:00 a.m. Be on the bus at 8:00."

Then I heard about Grand Circle Travel, designed for people over 50, and I read one of their brochures. What struck my eye was a trip that had one week in a hotel in Sorrento, Italy, and the next week in Tuscany. That meant only repacking the suitcase for one transfer. The more I read the better I liked it.

Sorrento is a town situated on the Amalfi Coast within an easy drive of many beautiful sights. Yes, there was a bus but it took us out each day to see a different part of the countryside. I was thankful for the skilled driver who shuttled us down the two-lane cliffside road of the Amalfi coastline, sheer

300 foot drop to the right, a wall of rock to left, and hairpin curves the entire trip. Without that bus, I would never have seen the exquisite village of Poisitano or shopped in the beautiful Ravella.

Another thing I would have missed without group travel was the wonderful interaction with people from so many diverse places. Getting to hear stories about their background and their travel experiences proved to be highly beneficial, even opening up future travel options that they would recommend. Also our program directors who traveled with us were a source of delight. They are chosen for their ability to enlighten their guests about the history, geography, and culture of the locale we visited. On that first trip to Italy our director, Susie, was fascinated by the four of us who were sketching and painting along the way. She asked Diane (an art instructor) if she would be willing to offer a session as a part of the "Discovery Series" for those who were interested in painting. Here is Susie, very seriously absorbing Dianne's lesson on perspective.

At the end of the first week our bus transferred us to Montecatini in the heart of Tuscany, where we stayed for the rest of trip. There were day trips to Florence, Sienna, Pisa and Lucca, some of the loveliest locations in the entire country. One day some of us took a train to Viareggio on the shore of the Mediterranean, just meandering around on our own. Of all my trips with Grand Circle, this was probably my favorite. There was a painting opportunity in every direction. Subject matter was abundant, but time constraints limited the number of sketches I could finish.

An unusually modern church in the Tuscan town of Montecatini

On the long trip from Sorrento to Tuscany, several of us learned that we enjoyed playing bridge. We managed to find a cardboard box that could be wedged in the aisle between seats to serve as a bridge table. We then positioned ourselves, two on each side, and kept a running bridge game going for the entire trip. Bus travel CAN be fun.

Another opportunity to unpack only one time was again with Grand Circle, this time on a cruise. I am NOT a fan of cruises, as a rule. Sailing on a ship through the Caribbean, entertaining ourselves with food and evening floor shows, and occasionally dropping into a tropical port just isn't my notion of fun. But traveling through the heart of Europe on a small riverboat (120 passengers) is an entirely different experience.

We flew into Amsterdam where we had one day to tour the city and visit the Ann Frank museum after moving into our cabins aboard ship. This cruise began on the Main River, traveling 647 miles into the Rhine and Danube Rivers before reaching Vienna.

One after another we saw beautiful vineyards, with the rows planted vertically on the side of the sloping fields. I soon learned the reason: the vines get sunshine more equally than if the rows were horizontal.

And at every bend in the river stood another magnificent castle.

Traveling through the innumerable locks was fascinating to me because I had no understanding of how they allowed ships to move from lower to higher elevations. After dinner one evening we sat on the sun deck to watch the entering and rising of water in this eighty-two foot lock. Captain Brandt was steering the ship manually through the concrete walls with about six inches to spare on either side.

The sun deck of our ship was a favorite place to sketch as we sailed through gorgeous countryside, dotted with ancient castles and small villages. Breathtaking views inspired us to paint and journal, thus affording me one of my favorite sketchbooks.

Passau on the Danube

Another ship experience that was delightful began in Vancouver, British Columbia, to travel through the Inside Passage of Alaska. The scenery changed constantly as the ship slowly maneuvered its way through the narrow straits and numerous islands. The breathtaking beauty was awe inspiring and provided non-stop entertainment for me from the observation area on Deck 12. I could read a book or write in a journal while absorbing the wonders of nature. Watching dolphins off the bow of the ship and seeing seals sun on the rocks at the shoreline was fascinating. One evening we spotted an Orca whale about 10 p.m., just before it got too dark to see.

Coming within half a mile of the Hubbard Glacier gave us a spectacular show as the sun came out and the glacier began to "calve." Huge chunks of ice would break and fall into the sea with the sound of thunder. On the ice in front of the glacier were hundreds of brown seals, sunning. As the captain brought the ship broadside he told us to watch and listen; because the weather conditions were perfect, this was the closest he had been able to approach the glacier.

On the trip to Alaska we took a side trip traveling by train into the Yukon territory. Spectacular scenery and riding on the totally authentic narrow gauge railroad made for a very fun day.

The one aggravating note was the aggressive Japanese tourist who stood on the platform **the entire trip** videotaping the passing sights. It never occurred to him to allow room for someone else to come out to take an occasional snapshot.

Buses, ships, planes, even one trip on a train, all have their pros and cons. But in 2009 I happened on a company that allowed you to "do it yourself." It is appropriately named "Untours" because they do NOT take you on a tour. Here's the way it works: The company has access to apartments of various sizes in numerous countries. On their website it is possible to select a destination and then review all the options available, including virtual tours of the lodgings. If desired, they rent a car and have it available at the airport upon arrival.

In Italy we were led by car to our agritourismo apartment near Trevi in Umbria. A "hostess" contacted us that day and explained that she would be meeting us for our first outing the next morning. At that time she gave us an in-depth look at the area, travel guides, maps and recommendations for sightseeing, everything we needed to design our own schedule. Our kitchen was stocked with food for the first evening meal and breakfast the next morning; afterward, we would purchase groceries at a local supermarket. The amount of food for the first day lasted us much longer than that.

I would not hesitate to take another Untours trip because the freedom of choosing your agenda is liberating. Each evening we would study maps and travel guides to prepare for the next day's adventures.

The downside of this experience is the need to drive a manual transmission car, in a foreign country, while trying to interpret maps and road signs. Sue was our designated driver and did a masterful job, but it definitely interfered with her ability to enjoy the journey.

In the Umbrian countryside

I have also planned trips with very little help from outside, just choosing a destination, making hotel reservations and travel arrangements myself. The first trip that Sue and I took was to New England in 1988, flying into Boston, renting a car and meandering through Maine, New Hampshire and Vermont before returning to Massachusetts to the airport. Having the opportunity to witness the spectacular scenery at the height of "color season" in October was truly a powerful experience. At every bend in the road, Sue would declare, "It is simply breathtaking!" and it was.

Sign at the foot of "Old Man in the Mountain"

So for me it is not either/or but both/and. I have loved all my trips, some more than others, but each one has its good points and a few minor disappointments. I cannot truthfully say which type of trip I prefer; I have to wait until the next possibility presents itself to decide if this is one I want to pursue.

Chapter 11
Stopping to Smell the Roses

"The real voyage of discovery consists not in seeking new landscapes, but in having new eyes."
— *Marcel Proust*

I found the following words in one of my old journals that I had written in March 1999: I was spending time on Lake Louisa with Larry and Sue at their Florida lake house.

"From my bedroom window facing east, the sky is pink, purple and blue-grey. The colors are mirrored in the glassy lake. Then something quite big flies to a middle branch of a nearby tree; everything is in silhouette against the multi-colored sky. The large bird flies to another limb and the great round head tells me it's an owl.

"The colors change rapidly, becoming bright pink, and then a clear red sun peeks up behind the boathouse. Within 15 minutes all the pink is gone and piercing yellow-white sunlight is blazing onto the lake, creating a reflection which is as bright as the sun itself.

"And everything else — cypress trees, moss, piers, boats, rooflines — all are shades of black and grey. Even the lake is silver-grey except for the white hot glare that shimmers, moves, changes with the ripples of the water. So much beauty; such rapid change."

It is so easy to get caught up in the moment when we travel and fail to absorb the beauty around us. I had forgotten about that journal entry, but rereading it brought back the sensations of that early morning in F.lorida.

Sunset on another day on Lake Louisa

When traveling in the Northwest from one national park to the next, one of the stops on the tour was at Jackson Lake Lodge south of Yellowstone. After lunch there was time to wander about the grounds, breathe the cool fresh air and gaze across the lake at the mountains. There was also time to capture this view which dominated the landscape behind the lodge. Majestic is too mild a word to describe these awesome mountains.

The Grand Tetons

Another extraordinary experience occurred in the Ozark mountains where we were attending an artist Elderhostel. After eating dinner one evening at a local restaurant, we had to wait a while to leave because of the heavy downpour. Suddenly it stopped. Just as we exited the building, a full double arc rainbow appeared immediately in front of us. This was the first time I had seen such a thing; I had no idea that the colors are reversed in a double arc: violet, blue, green, yellow, orange, red; then red, orange, yellow, green, blue, violet.

After never having seen a double rainbow I was delighted to see my second one from our apartment window in Murlo, Italy in 2009.

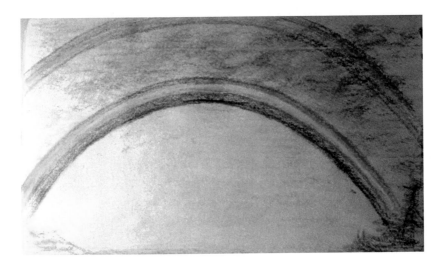

When four of us traveled to New York in 2007 we took in all the usual sights, saw some plays (*Curtains* and *Wicked*), had free cosmetic makeovers in Saks, and walked miles and miles. On Sunday as we discussed how to spend that day, it was obvious that the other three wanted to take the Staten Island Ferry to visit the Statue of Liberty, but that didn't particularly appeal to me. I encouraged them to go without me, choosing to attend Fifth Avenue Presbyterian Church to enjoy the magnificent music.

I was not disappointed; the two anthems were "Alleluia" by Randall Thompson and "Prayer to Jesus" by George Oldroyd. After the service I bought a hot pretzel from a street vendor and made my way to 53rd Street to the Museum of Modern Art.

72

This museum, MOMA, had been closed for renovation on my other trips to NYC and just recently reopened. I was overwhelmed by the visual feast, each gallery more spectacular than the one before. Being alone I could wander at my own pace, sketching, making notes, taking photographs, and drinking in the beauty. How thrilling to see Van Gogh's "*Olive Trees*" from the orchard at St. Remy, France, knowing that a few years before I had stood gazing at those same trees. It is impossible to describe the impact of seeing a Monet painting in person, but to look at "*Reflections of Clouds on Water,*" 8 feet tall and 45 feet wide, is mind boggling. In my journal I noted: "On that day my soul was fed in numerous ways."

Although I haven't been interested in taking an overseas trip alone, I have never hesitated to take long road trips by myself. Since I have a tendency to get drowsy from time to time, I fortify myself with large cups of ice and a good audio book to keep me awake. One such trip was from Columbia, South Carolina, to Berkeley Springs, West Virginia, in 2003. Becky had invited four of us to enjoy her family's summer home there. Being in no hurry, I broke the trip into two days so that I could go through Boone, North Carolina, and see some sights in Virginia. As I approached Lexington, Virginia, I remembered being told that I should drive through the campus of VMI. It is very beautiful, austere and obviously military. Immediately next to it is Washington and Lee University, all red brick with columns, typically southern style architecture.

Rather than stick to interstates I took Lee Highway (Hwy 11) north and drank in the beauty of the countryside through the Shenandoah Valley. The medians are blanketed with poppies and day lilies, actual carpets of flowers. These folks really took to heart the admonition to "beautify America!"

During our stay in West Virginia we took a two-night side trip to Pennsylvania, touring the Gettysburg battlefield. The guides there are outstanding. At the cemetery we heard a "living history" presentation by a young history teacher who spends his summers as a tour guide. He took the persona of a union soldier who had come to visit the graves of his fellow soldiers. He concluded by playing a very moving rendition of "Amazing Grace" on his fife.

Gen. Warren overlooking the Gettysburg battlefield at the Round Top

Being so near Hershey, Pennsylvania, we had to see the chocolate factory. Their delightful "Chocolate World" tour consisted of a train ride through the chocolate-making demo, concluding with a free candy bar. Of course, on the way out was the gift shop where every kind of Hershey candy in the world was available for purchase.

The real highlight of the trip was riding through the Amish country. The roads crisscross the farms through corn and wheat fields, vegetable gardens, barns, cattle, horses and silos. There is always a very large farm house with exquisitely landscaped yard, and even gorgeous flower beds lining the vegetable gardens.

Seeing the buggies making their way in the midst of all the vehicle traffic was very much as we had pictured. But the entire country gives a more affluent impression than we had expected.

They still dry their laundry in the sun.

Chapter 12
Getting Lost and Living to Tell About It

"Not all those who wander are lost."
—J.R.R. Tolkien

What would be the fun of travel if you couldn't bring home stories of your adventures, even if they had to be exaggerated sometimes in the telling. My stories of getting lost don't need to be inflated, however. They really happened like this:

In 2009 four of us (Ellen Gunn, Phyllis Parker, Sue Spitchley and I) made the trip to Italy with Untours. With a very nice station wagon and Sue as the driver, we set out on our first morning with the directions in hand to meet our hostess at an Umbrian agritourismo (farm with guest accommodations). Even though I consider myself a pretty good navigator, the little roads and villages, foreign road signs, and an Italian map gave me fits. We turned around three or four times as we made our way, arriving at the farm ten minutes late. Upon leaving we made another wrong turn on the farm road before we could make it back to the highway. This was a precursor of the rest of our "do-it-yourself" trip.

Our Agritourismo, Il Casa Grande

Later that week we took a day trip to Todi and on to Orvieto in the afternoon. We had learned that there would be a 5 p.m. concert by a youth orchestra in the Duomo there. On our return trip (almost two hours back to our apartment) we took an exit that put us on a country road which dead ended in a pig farmer's front yard. We pulled to a stop and saw another car turning around headed out, also lost. As I tried to ask for directions with *no Italiano* to the farmer with *no Inglese,* we jabbered back and forth, looking at the map, pointing up the road, with little understanding on either side. My three companions were in the car giggling. As he repeatedly pointed at our gas tank, it dawned on me that he was indicating a place to buy gas, thus a landmark further along. Eventually I got enough information to get us back on the right road to Il Casa Grande before nightfall.

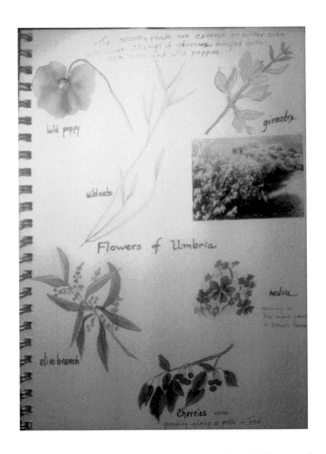

The roadsides through the country are covered with huge clumps of ginestre, mingled with sea oats and wild poppies

And so it went...Umbria and Tuscany...then time to return to Rome for our flight home the next day. Our new friends, Dino and Laura (a college friend of Marietta's) who had given us a tour of Cortona earlier in the week, realized that we were very nervous about driving into Rome and delivering the rental car at the airport. They offered to accompany us, Dino driving our car with Sue and Ellen, Laura taking Phyllis and me on the train. Upon debarking we planned to use our map of Rome to get us to the hotel (big mistake!), but even though Laura can read and speak Italian, the three of us walked in circles for at least three miles. Finally connecting with Dino back at the train station, he put us in a taxi which got us to our destination.

At least we were together when we got lost in Italy. But getting lost **by myself** in Madrid was a different story. Our trip from Atlanta to Spain included a connection in Frankfurt where we stood in lo-o-o-ng security lines to clear passport control. The two hour flight to Madrid started with a screaming child whose mother kept whipping her to make her shut up! Arriving at the Hotel Tryp Cibeles on Gran Via (the main street of Madrid), we took naps before going out for a walking tour of the city center. By this time it had gotten dark but there were lots of people on the streets. Our program director, Victor Santos, was giving a running description of what we were seeing while we were snapping pictures along the way. At one stop I was trying to get a shot of a building inside a wrought iron fence, but upon turning around, my group was nowhere in sight. I looked on every side street, but saw no one that I recognized. At this point I told myself I should not panic because I knew the name of the hotel, and I could get a taxi to take me there. Also, I had a slip of paper with Victor's name and cell phone number in my pocket; he had handed them out before we left. (This is the only time I remember being given the phone number of the leader upon arriving in a country.)

I had no cell phone (that would work in Spain) but I began to look for someone who might help me. I noticed a middle-aged woman reach in her purse for her cellphone and before she could dial, I hurried over saying *"por favor"* (please). She looked at me, puzzled, as I put my fingers to my ear to signal "telephone." I handed her the slip of paper indicating that I was lost and needed to find my

group. She called Victor, who answered immediately. He told her where to find the group and said they would wait for me. With hand signals she was able to show me which way to walk to find them. At breakfast the next morning I thanked Victor for providing me with the phone number.

He said, "It was good. You didn't panic. Some people would call the police and go back to U. S."

My first trip to France was with Ellen, Sue and Kay Adkins in 2000. We were traveling with the handbell choir from the University of Southern Mississippi. They played concerts in many venues on this trip, starting with one on Sunday afternoon at the American Church. After the concert, the bus took everyone to the Eiffel Tower so they could climb to the top. Ellen decided to make the climb but Sue, Kay and I chose to walk and eat our picnic while we waited. It was very cool by the Seine, so we started walking back to find the bus and wait for the group out of the cold. Kay looked ahead and said, "There's a Meyers' bus" (the name of our bus company) and I said, "but it can't be ours because it's full of people and they are leaving." That's when we noticed everyone on the bus waving frantically. When they couldn't get tickets to the tower, **they just got back on the bus and drove away!** Ellen was saying, "Please don't leave my friends." At that point, the bus began to circle so everyone could search the crowds for three women who did not know they were lost!

Technically, getting separated from a tour group in London did not mean that we were **lost**, but it was very, very annoying since we thought it was someone else's fault. On a trip to England in 2010, a fellow art student and I decided to take a day tour of London. The bus took us by many of the famous sights, also touring inside St. Paul's Cathedral and the Tower of London. From there we took a boat trip on the Thames, just riding and looking at Big Ben and the London Eye along the way. My friend and I were sitting near the front of the boat when we realized that we didn't see anyone we recognized. We asked a crew member about the tour group; he said that some people got off the

boat at the last stop (apparently from the back of the boat). We had no choice but to continue on the river until the next stop, then walk a half mile to the closest underground station that took us back to our hotel in Kensington.

This was my second time that a tour guide failed to "count heads." **And** since I had intended to return to the bus, I left my sketchbook in my seat. Thankfully, it was early in the trip and I hadn't done much work in it, but I had to get another one before our art classes started the next day.

In the sketch, the handwritten text reads:

Crest Hall
Ivy Covered Cottage
In Cathedral Square
Durham
—— house dates from end of 13th c

*In Cathedral Square in Durham, UK, this ivy covered cottage
dates from the end of the 13th century*

My friend Marian said to me recently that she would hesitate to travel with me, considering all my stories of getting "lost." And yet, none of those experiences made me afraid to travel; keeping cool, using good sense, and paying attention has always paid off for me. Also, not hesitating to seek help from strangers and receiving kindness in return has been a worthwhile lesson.

Chapter 13
Lucky Loser

"It takes a long time to become young."
—Pablo Picasso

As a child my mother stayed frustrated with me for being so careless with my belongings. I lost everything from wallets to umbrellas because I didn't pay attention to what I was doing. Unfortunately, that trait followed me to adulthood and has created some dicey situations from time to time.

Leaving Mobile after a three-day visit with our little bridge group at Kay Adkins' home, I decided to stop at Fresh Market on my way out of town. I made my purchases and headed back to Georgia. After driving about 17 miles, I reached over to get something from my purse only to see that I had NO purse. I still had my cellphone, so I quickly called the store to see if I had left it there. Yes, they had it…a lady found it in the parking lot still in the grocery cart where my car had been parked. "Thank you, God, for people who are honest."

Just a few months ago I decided that I needed to investigate the "Find My iPhone" app. It had to be downloaded to all my devices and identified as such so I set it up on iPhone and iPad. Merely 3 days later I decided to stop for brunch at the IHOP restaurant on my way home from Marietta's house on Easter Sunday morning after early church. Since there was such a long waiting list at that location, I decided to continue to the IHOP in Hiram. After finishing my brunch and returning to my apartment, I looked for my cell phone but it was nowhere to be found. Immediately opening the app on my iPad, it pinpointed the first IHOP on a map. When I called they said that an iPhone had been found in their parking lot and turned in. But two weeks later I left it in Marietta's living room; the app showed me that it was on South Sherwood. I'd had this phone for over a year without downloading the app, then I needed it twice in the the month after adding "Find my iPhone." As I said, "I am a lucky loser."

My sketchbooks are such a prized possession that I try to take extra care with them when I travel. But after trying on hats and purchasing one in a shop in Montalcino, Italy, I was several blocks away when I realized that I didn't have my sketchbook with me. Retracing my steps to the gift shop, I found my book on the shelf beside the hat rack.

While visiting Betty and Sinclair Lewis in Ireland, we took a fun trip to Blarney Castle where of course we had to climb to the top in order to kiss the Blarney stone. (No one had told me that you had to lie down backwards to kiss it.) But as we started to climb down, I dropped my camera from a parapet near the top of the castle. Seeing someone nearby on the ground, I called out to the man to pick up my camera. He graciously agreed, left it at the gift shop, and I continued to take pictures without a hitch.

Probably the most traumatic loss was when we took a day trip to Malaga, Spain, spending the day at the open air market and visiting another Picasso museum. (I took that opportunity to copy one of his famous abstract paintings.)

But my day took a turn for the worst. Our trip concluded in a small cafe, *Casa Aranda,* where we enjoyed chocolate and churros (fried pastry). The

Bust of a Woman Wearing
a Striped Hat
1939

bus took us back to our hotel in Torremolinos before I discovered that my purse was missing. I talked with Victor, our director, speculating that I had it at our last stop at the cafe. He called the restaurant for me, explained that our group had been in a private dining room upstairs, and they promised to look for it. Later he called again to learn that it had been found on the floor under a table. By this time I had cancelled my credit cards, but I was encouraged because other travelers told me later that they had prayed for me to St. Anthony, patron saint of lost things.

The next day was a free day for us because we decided not to go on the optional tour to Morocco. Since Malaga was 15 miles away, we got very good directions on how to take the train and walk to the restaurant. When I walked into the busy Sunday morning rush hour at *Casa Aranda*, the owner insisted on identification before opening his safe to retrieve my red purse.

Ellen, who has been with me on several of those occasions, suggested that I needed to devote a page to purses in my sketchbook.

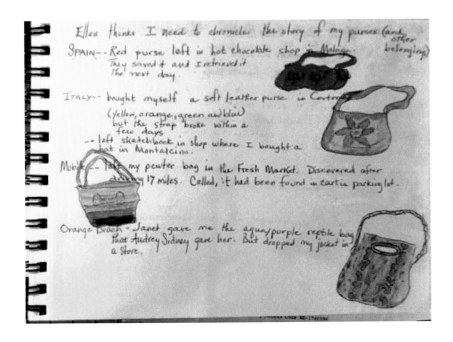

Ellen thinks I need to chronicle the story of my purses (and other belonging)

SPAIN -- Red purse left in hot chocolate shop in Malaga. They saved it and I retrieved it the next day.

ITALY -- bought myself a soft leather purse in Cortona (yellow, orange, green and blue) but the strap broke within a few days
-- left sketchbook in shop where I bought a hat in Montalcino.

Mobile -- left my pewter bag in the Fresh Market. Discovered after driving 17 miles. Called, it had been found in cart in parking lot.

Orange Beach - Janet gave me the aqua/purple reptile bag that Audrey Sidney gave her. But dropped my jacket in a store.

Chapter 14
Stuff Just Happens When You Are Out and About

"Expecting the world to treat you fairly because you are a good person is like expecting the bull not to charge you because you are a vegetarian."

—*Rabbi Harold Kushner*

One of the small pleasures of keeping a journal when you travel is having a record of little unexpected adventures. They are easy to forget but so much fun to recall.

For instance, while a friend and I were sketching the lovely fountain in the plaza of St. Paul de Vence, France, I sat on a low concrete wall beside the main walkway. A big black dog, out for a walk with its owner, came over to observe my work. He moved so close that his head hung over my sketchbook. When he walked away, I noticed that

he had drooled on the page where I was painting. I made a note in the book about the incident and continued to paint. Noticing what had happened, an Australian lady spoke up: "They have rabies in France" to which Diane replied "Thanks a lot!" "No charge," the lady said.

At the same location that morning, a group of Japanese tourists noticed Diane and me at work and requested that we allow them to be photographed "with the artists." Somewhere in Japan, two unidentified American women have a place in someone's photo album.

A few years before, Larry and Sue had been to France and were enchanted with this beautiful village a few miles north of the Mediterranean Sea. After our trip to St. Paul, with my sketches and photographs, I was able to paint the Grande Fountaine on Rue Grande as my Christmas gift to them after we returned.

Another brush with an animal occurred during a trip to Spain. Our tour group was waiting to enter the Cathedral of Seville, standing alongside a horse-drawn carriage. As we inched forward I was sketching and making notes in my journal, paying no attention to how close I was to the horse. Suddenly, he turned and chomped down on the corner of my sketchbook. The teethmarks can still be seen at the edge of the page.

In 2000 when we were in Lucerne, Switzerland, I fell down the steps as we exited the Picasso museum. I was not hurt but I was dismayed to see that I had broken one of the four little mugs that I bought earlier in the afternoon. Since this was to be a gift for a Jackson friend, I couldn't take home just three mugs. I knew how to find the store where they were bought, but on the way we had to duck in a candy store to avoid the sudden hail storm that erupted. When I finally arrived at the Bodum store, they had closed for the day. By pecking on the window I attracted the attention of the clerk and showed her my broken cup. I had my euros in my hand and convinced her to open up and let me purchase one matching cup. Marilyn is still serving me coffee in those cups when I visit her.

A delightful surprise entertained us as we made our way through the Alps from Salzburg to Vienna. Having toured all the locations in Salzburg that were filmed for *"Sound of Music,"* it was great fun to watch the movie on the bus the next morning. We recognized the fortress, Mozart Square, the abbey, and the cemetery where the family hid from the Germans. Just outside Salzburg the bus stopped at Mondsee (Moon Lake) to see the chapel where the Von Trapp wedding scene was filmed. It is a picture-postcard village and the church is gorgeous. Reportedly, the film crew decorated the interior of the church to resemble the one in Salzburg where the wedding was actually performed, but eventually the locals grew tired of the disturbance and asked "Hollywood" to move their filming elsewhere.

On at least four trips we have joined Grand Circle Travel for their guided tours. On each trip you have a program director who makes all arrangements and also serves as an educational guide to provide history and cultural enrichment to the tourists. In my opinion, our very best director was Ralph Waugh, who guided us through Nova Scotia and the Canadian Maritimes in 2004. As a former music video producer, he had a wealth of stories to share about famous Canadians such as Anne Murray and

Celine Dion. He also had documentary videos that he played for us on our lengthy bus ride to make the travel more interesting.

Ralph had a rotation system on the bus that added so much to the trip. On our first day he made name cards for the seats we had chosen and every day we moved those cards one row up or back so that a different couple always sat across the aisle from us. This also meant that two different people were sitting on the front seats to his right. During the day he would ask those people to speak over the bus loud speaker about themselves and their home states. Little by little, we learned something about everyone of our fellow travelers.

Prior to the trip, Ralph had loaded his MP3 player with a huge variety of music so that he could quickly choose appropriate music for any occasion. When the designated speaker for the day finished talking, he would play a song representing their state or part of the country, such as the Cornhusker fight song for Nebraska, "Chicago" for the Illinois couple, "Rocky Mountain High" for the folks from Colorado, and "Mississippi Mud" for Sue and me.

A tall ship in the harbor at Ralph's home town, Halifax.

On our guided tour around London in 2010 the tour guide showed us the Lanesborough Hotel where members of the Qatari royal family were staying. Their three bedroom suite reportedly cost £ 3500 per night. In front of the hotel we saw their turquoise Swedish sports car (a Koenigsegg,

cost £ 1.2 mil). The tour guide explained that Ali Fayed had recently sold Harrod's department store to the royal family of Qatar for a half billion pounds. The day before our tour, one of the Qatari royals had parked the sports car directly in front of Harrods; their status didn't impress the police who promptly impounded it for illegal parking!

In 2005 we cruised the Great Rivers of Europe from Amsterdam to Vienna, down the Main River to the Rhine and through the Danube. When we docked in Bamberg, Germany, each tourist was given € 2 (two euros) and instructed to buy German pastries, kuchen, cheese cake, etc. for our afternoon Kaffee Klatsche on the ship. At 5 p.m. we

gathered for an incredible array of fruit, chocolate, and nutty sweets which covered two tables in the lounge. A glutton's delight! But at 6:30 we were in the dining room again for dinner. Not perfect scheduling!

Learning to adapt to the food in foreign countries is sometimes a challenge. Never more so than when we order coffee. As explained earlier, I always learned to say "hot water" in the language of the country I visited, just so that I could weaken the coffee enough to drink it. But in our apartment in Italy where we had our own kitchen, arising early, I was the coffee maker each morning. At that time, I had never seen anything like the pot that we were expected to use. Non-electric, in three parts, the bottom section was filled with water, the middle section was filled with very finely ground expresso and screwed to the bottom section. The top portion of the pot received the coffee that bubbled up as the little pot boiled on the gas burners.

Immediately upon tasting, I realized that it was stronger than any Starbucks offering so I devised a plan. At the time I started the coffee, I also started a pot of water boiling. Filling our cups with half hot water and the rest with espresso made it perfectly drinkable.

What are the chances that you will run into someone in a distant country that you enjoyed meeting the first time you were there? I had told our Untours group when we decided to go to Sienna, Italy, that my very favorite local guide was the young woman who showed us that beautiful ancient city. I remembered her name, Chiara, because she was the most enthusiastic, vivacious person that I had encountered. That day as we strolled through the city, I saw a group of tourists listening intently to their leader. Recognizing Chiara, I hastened over to speak and she graciously agreed to a photograph. She even pretended to remember me.

Chapter 15
Seven Parks in Seventeen Days

"If It's Tuesday, This Must Be Belgium"
Movie title from 1969

I had heard my sister-in-law say from time to time that she had always wanted to travel out west but had never had the opportunity. I had always thought that traveling with Sue and Larry would be lots of fun, so I approached Larry with a plan to surprise Sue at Christmas 2005. The two of us registered with Grand Circle Travel to take their

Seven Parks
Five States
Seventeen Days

tour of America's Majestic National Parks. Sue Spitchley came on board as my roommate and the four of us embarked in late June 2006.

Flying into Rapid City, South Dakota, we met the group and began the very long bus ride through five western states: South Dakota, Wyoming, Utah, Arizona and Colorado. I know that we were scheduled to see seven national parks, but it was hard to know when we moved from one to the next. Rather than enumerate them, I will just string together some stories and pictures that appealed to me on this trip.

Beside a waterfall in Yellowstone

Winding through the Black Hills of South Dakota, we arrived at the marvelous Crazy Horse Memorial, a fairly recent sculpture in the mountainside. Dedicated by the

100

sculptor Korczak Ziolkowski and Lakota Chief Henry Standing Bear in 1948 as a memorial to American Indians, only the head of the statue has been completed. Even so, its magnificence draws crowds to the visitor's center at the base of the mountain. Korczak worked on the project until his death in 1982 and in all his many years he refused to take any salary or accept government money for the project. After his death, his wife and ten children have continued pursuing the dream and now the grandchildren are involved.

The model shows the final plan for the statue, as it sits in plain view of the carving on the mountain

Although we also traveled on to Mount Rushmore, the much more famous carving of four U.S. presidents, it was not a bit more impressive than Crazy Horse with its inspiring ode to the human spirit and the dedication of one man and his family.

Still in the Black Hills we entered Wyoming to see Devil's Tower, a geologic feature that protrudes out of the rolling prairie and is considered sacred to the Lakota and other tribes with a connection to the area. The primary emotion as we traveled from one natural phenomenon to another was "awe." Pictures cannot possibly do justice to these features in the landscape that could never have been fashioned by human hands, but sketching them was immensely satisfying. And so we went from one magnificent view to the next.

Devil's Tower

The Watchman
in Zion National Park

Thor's Hammer in Bryce Canyon

The Watchman in Zion National Park

Monument Valley, located on the Arizona-Utah border

This unusual rugged landscape was made famous first in director John Ford's movies, beginning with "*Stagecoach*," in 1939 starring John Wayne. It became a favorite location for films of the Old West and is readily recognized even by people who may not know the name. I made this sketch standing in front of Goulding's Trading Post, whose original owner, Harry Goulding, introduced John Ford to Monument Valley.

As we headed into Wyoming, I learned that our lunch stop that day would be "Dirty Annie's," an isolated cafe that my daughter had described from their stay at a working dude ranch in the vicinity. When I told her where we were, apparently she called the ranch and told someone that her mother would be there that day, because as we were finished eating, I heard my name being called. When I answered, the waitress said "There's a man at the front door asking for you." To my surprise, one of their wrangler friends had come by to meet me and send greetings to Marietta and Pat. Stuart showed me the outline of the buildings on their ranch across the highway, which could be clearly seen from the front porch of the cafe. Everyone on the bus enjoyed seeing a "real cowboy."

Speaking of real cowboys, we attended the rodeo when we arrived in Cody, Wyoming. It was my first rodeo and it sure felt authentic to me. Not much glitz and glitter, just lots of action. Some of the action wasn't in the ring, however. As we sat a few rows above the bull pen, we noticed the riders preparing to mount their bulls.

One guy was really working hard to get ready. Wearing a black Stetson and lime green shirt, collar turned up, he stretched his legs and his shoulders in one direction and then the other, lifting each leg to the top of the railing.

He must have known how good looking he was and that all the women were watching him (Sue, Mary Sue and I certainly were), because he preened and postured at length. At last it was his turn to ride. The bull must not have been impressed with his handsome rider, however, because he threw him off by the time they cleared the pen.

Our accommodations in Jackson Hole, Wyoming, were at the Snake River Lodge and Spa. As we entered our room we gasped upon being greeted by a life-size black bear perched on the railing of our balcony. Later we saw these same whimsical statues peeking around corners and behind bushes throughout the grounds.

The Snake River was the one disappointment on this trip. We had signed up for a rafting trip, thinking that it would be a great adventure. The weather was overcast, threatening rain, but the excursion proceeded. At the outset we were provided life jackets and ponchos, which should have been a signal of what was to come. As we moved slowly down the flat, featureless Snake River, we were eager to see wildlife or beautiful scenery but alas, there was

neither. The clouds gathered and the drizzle began, so we donned our ponchos.

This totally unpleasant boat ride seemed endless as the rain began to pound. We were looking forward to getting

off the river for the promised barbecue meal at the end of the journey.

But the barbecue was as disappointing as the river trip: a roadside joint with wooden tables outside served mediocre food on paper plates.

However, this experience didn't dampen our enthusiasm for the rest of our trip.   In Utah we enjoyed seeing the beautiful Mormon Tabernacle in Salt Lake City. Although non-Mormons do not enter that space, there is a large building that houses the "Family Search Center," a computer center for genealogy research.   Each of us took a different branch of our family to investigate, even though we didn't get very far with the Dunaways and Pyrons.   There were young people who would assist with your search if needed, and we realized that they were probably a type of missionary who would engage in conversation about their faith. One young woman, who indicated that she was in the States from Hong Kong, was very assertive in instructing Larry about the truth of her religion. In his broad Mississippi accent, Larry was just as vocal in explaining the truth of his Baptist faith. Not to be deterred, she pressed forward, but Larry was adamant about his beliefs. The exchange became

almost comical with her soft Asian accent and his rugged southern drawl; eventually she gave up, apparently convinced that she would never make a convert of him.

My favorite sight on the entire trip was the tour through Antelope Canyon near the Arizona/Utah border. The walls are ribboned layers of brilliant color, in every conceivable shade of red. I have attempted to paint from my photographs to approximate the stunning experience, but it defies my best efforts.

Certainly a picture cannot convey its beauty, but at least I can suggest how it looked.

Our tour ended on Larry's birthday, July 6, with a farewell dinner for the entire group. At one of the gift shops we found a t-shirt for his birthday gift with the following inscription:

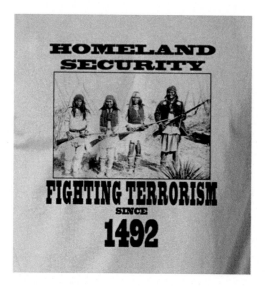

ChispaClothingLLC©2009

Chapter 16
Italia the Beautiful

"Open my heart and you will see
Graven inside of it, "Italy"
—Robert Browning

When I am traveling I usually fall in love with what I am seeing and experiencing at the time. I do my best to be a good tourist and appreciate each country for its unique features. I want to learn everything I can about each culture and be respectful of the values and practices of the place I am visiting.

And yet it is not surprising that some places make more of an impact than others; I remember more about them and relish the memories more fully. That is certainly true of my two trips to Italy. I read those sketchbooks more often and recollect the events more completely. Maybe it has something to do with the food: authentic Italian food is at the top of my all time favorites list.

Italy is truly unforgettable. Even with the language barrier, the people are so easy to get to know. They are genuinely friendly, helpful and enthusiastic about visitors to their country. There may not be time for me to make another trip to Italy because there are so many other places to visit, but I doubt that it will be replaced as my favorite.

Gate in beautiful Montefalco, Italy

Little details that we learned are still fresh in my mind, like rose bushes at the end of every row in the vineyards. When I asked why, I learned that the growers can check the roses for insects to alert them to the need for insecticide. For me, their beautiful blooms would have been reason enough.

Shopping in the nearby supermarket when we arrived was an enlightening experience. One must NEVER touch the produce. I couldn't imagine not being able to check to see if the tomato was firm or if the apples had bruises. But I was quickly admonished by the worker who was watching my every movement.

Our tiny Tuscan village of Murlo has only 15 permanent residents, but the ancient town is home to a fine Etruscan museum. We learned that the area had been occupied as early as 7th century B.C. before being destroyed by fire. Artifacts have been discovered from the 5th century B.C. which indicate a very advanced lifestyle with art, architecture, implements and utensils in bronze, terra cotta, gold and jade. What a gem nestled in the hills of Tuscany!

In the above photo of the village, the apartment where we lived can be seen at the top left (marked with X).

could look out our living room window onto the courtyard. (My sketch from that window is on the front cover of this book.)   On the back of the apartment was a tiny terrace overlooking distant villages and farmland.

The only entrance to the village was through an arched gateway in the surrounding wall. Maneuvering our station wagon up the hill to turn right through the gate in order to unload our heavy luggage was a major feat. Cars had to be parked outside down the hill.

I mentioned the wonderful food and a few specifics come to mind. In Murlo there was a restaurant across the courtyard. After a weary day of touring, we decided to eat out instead of cooking. Just a small pizza would be fine, so we each ordered one. When it arrived, the crisp edges were hanging off the large dinner plate and the total price was only € 4.

It didn't take long for us to discover gelato and we quickly realized that a gelateria was a perfect place for our rest stop at 3 p.m. each afternoon. We would each choose a different flavor: mint, lemon, pineapple, chocolate/cherry, so we could share and sample. There were too many to finish them all during our visit.

Molto buono!

What you may have heard about Italian men is mostly true; they are a delight for the eyes. During an evening stroll we found a tiny community called Azzano, consisting of three homes, a church and a little store where a few men were circled around "chewing the fat." They graciously agreed to pose for a picture as we were leaving.

Men gather at the store in Azzano to visit and gossip.

But my study of Italian men would not be complete without a picture of younger men as well. While eating in a sandwich shop, several cute guys took a seat near us. I

immediately pulled out my camera, while my friends were saying, "You can't take pictures of other people without permission!" Not to be deterred, I aimed at our table while my friends posed for me; then I tilted my camera up just enough to capture the young men (without asking permission).

My two favorite towns in Tuscany are Lucca and Sienna. Both are very old, well preserved, walled cities. There are so many interesting stories to be learned when we walk through these cities with a local tour guide. For

instance, in Lucca there is a very tall square tower covered with trees on the flat roof. The story goes that the mayor of the city had decreed that no tower could exceed the height of those already built. Not to be outdone, the family who built this tower planted trees on the roof to declare their wealth and power.

The story from Sienna is even more fascinating. Twice every year a horse race called The Palio is held in the Il Campo piazza or central square. A dirt track is built around the top of the square, higher than the recessed center where the people stand shoulder to shoulder. A friend said that the infield at the

Palio is so crowded you could faint and not fall down. Hours to wait and no bathroom! Because the square is shaped like a shell, the race around the upper track can be seen by all. The rivalry between the seventeen districts in the city is intense for a bareback horse race lasting 1 minute, 15 seconds. The first horse across the finish line wins, **with or without** the rider.

Even without stories, the pictures and sketches from these trips continue to enthrall me. Photo opps and painting locales call out at every turn. For instance, newly arrived in Umbria we drove about a mile from our apartment when suddenly, looming ahead just off the highway, we saw the hilltop town of Trevi. To me it epitomized the typical landscape of rural Italy.

Sketched from the side of the highway

And while strolling through Cortona we noticed that a wedding was about to begin. But what a surprise to see this member of the wedding party:

Everyone knows that visiting churches and monasteries is mandatory for viewing architecture, art, and history in a country like Italy. But some of them are truly memorable. Touring the Abbey of Monte Orvieto, founded in 1319 a.d., we viewed frescoes by Signorelli (15th C.) depicting the life of St. Benedict. They stretched the entire length and width of the central courtyard.

Drawbridge at the entrance to the Abbey

One other abbey captured my interest because we wanted to hear the "singing of the hours" by the monks. We had lunch in the charming town of Montalcino before driving into the countryside nearby to find the abbey. Arriving at 2:45 we took our places in the chapel of the Abbazia de Sant Antimo for the celebration of None (mid-afternoon prayer). Eight monks clad in white robes entered the sanctuary and sang in Latin, a cappella, for about fifteen minutes. It was ethereally beautiful.

Sometimes when touring there isn't enough time to complete a sketch with the detail it needs. At times like that I often make a collage, incorporating photos in a setting that I paint.

Here are two of these types of entries from our visit to Assisi, home of St. Francis.

And I surely must include my sketch of the Leaning Tower, after the innumerable pictures I have seen of this phenomenon. A trip to Pisa should be a requisite for any Tuscan visitor.

There are many more stories and more pictures of this magical country. But my memory is getting shorter so I am recording these few to remind me of my genuine appreciation for the people who have preserved this beauty for the rest of us to enjoy.

Chapter 17
And In Conclusion....

Don't cry because it's over; smile because it happened."
— Dr. Seuss

When I was preparing to retire at the end of 1994, one question that I asked my financial planner was "Will I be able to take at least one nice trip each year?" He assured me that, if we included this expense in my overall budget, he believed that I could continue to travel as long as my health was good. That reassurance made me more confident in my decision to quit work because I had been dreaming about exploring new sights and scenery my entire life.

In these twenty years I have managed to do so many of the things that appealed to me, from seeing more of my country to visiting European countries that I had only known from pictures. When I began gathering the material for this book, I was surprised to see just how much territory I have covered. I am very grateful for the financial ability to fulfill those dreams and for the continued good health that allows me to plan more trips in the near future.

I have never been to Scandinavia nor traveled through the Panama Canal. I long to spend time in the Greek Islands and to linger in the English countryside. Although I haven't been to Asia or South America maybe I need to think about that. But neither have I been to the Outer Banks of North Carolina, the Grand Canyon or the redwood forests of California. So much to see and so little time. However, I shall not despair; there is still time to cross a few of those items from my list.

This fall I will travel with RoadScholars (educational programs for senior citizens) to San Miguel de Allende, Mexico, a veritable artists' paradise.

There is still lots of time for more adventure....

Coast of Nova Scotia, 2004

Chronology of Major Trips

1995	Palaces Tour	St. Petersburg, Russia
1997	Visit with the Lewises	Cork, Ireland
1998	Inside Passage Cruise	Canada/Alaska
1999	Eldershostel	Ozark Mountains, AR
2000	Handbell Tour with USM	Paris to Vienna
2001	Art Trip with Maggie	Provence, FR
2003	Becky's Family House	WV and PA
2003	Grand Circle Travel	Tuscany/Amalfi Coast of Italy
2004	Grand Circle Bus Tour	Nova Scotia and Canadian Maritimes
2005	Great Rivers of Europe Cruise with GCT	Amsterdam to Vienna
2006	Nat'l Parks of Northwest	SD, WY, UT, AZ, CO
2007	Girl's Trip (4 of us)	New York
2007	Grand Circle Travel	Spain/ Portugal
2009	Untours (4 of us)	Umbria/ Tuscany
2010	Paint and Relax	Durham, UK
2013	Crystal Bridges Museum	Bentonville, AR
2014	San Miguel De Allende	Mexico

Trips with the W Bunch

Sep 1987	Lake Tiak O'Khata	Louisville, MS
Fall 1989	Lake Tiak O'Khata	Louisville, MS
July 1993	Old Edwards Inn	Highlands, NC
Aug 1995	J-3 Ranch	Starkville, MS
July 1998	Calloway Gardens	Pine Mountain, GA
July 1999	Sally's Home	Shelbyville, TN
July 2000	Geri's Home	Sautee, GA
July 2001	Gray Center	Canton, MS
July 2002	Long Beach House	Port St. Joe, FL
Mar 2003	Lewis' Tinnin East	Edisto Island, SC
Apr 2004	Clark's Condo	Orange Beach, AL
July 2005	Gray Center	Canton, MS
Jun 2006	Chamber's Lodge	Blowing Rock, NC
Jun 2007	Bear Cliff Village	Lake James, NC
Apr 2008	Long's Lake House	Pickwick Lake, MS
May 2009	Lewis' Tinnin East	Edisto Island, SC
Apr 2010	Clark's Condo	Orange Beach, AL
May 2011	Island House	Jekyll Island, GA
May 2012	Cinnamon Ridge B&B	Shelbyville, TN
May 2013	Martinique on the Gulf	Ft. Morgan, AL
Mar 2013	Plymouth Bluff	Columbus/Starkville, MS

W Bunch Roster

Class of 1958

Geri Barfield Ingram
Becky Perkins

Class of 1957

Nancy Virden Alford
Ellen Young Gunn
Jo Nell Thomas Hales
Beverly Koch Jones
Donette Dunaway Lee
Betty Ratliff Lewis
Sally Brockway McReynolds
Carolyn Smithson Ritter

Class of 1956

Sylvia Duck Clark
Ina Rae Aven Coggeshall
Barbara Garrett
Douglas Ann Stevens Graham
Nan McElroy Long
Janet Smith

Acknowledgments

Patient friends along the way gave me time and space to sketch and paint, at sidewalk cafes, standing in line at cathedrals, in our hotel rooms, and sitting on rocks by the seashore. I appreciate their encouraging me to pursue my art in the midst of hurry-scurry on the go.

I am indebted to Sally McReynolds for the use of her memorial talk at Plymouth Bluff. For proof reading and critiquing I owe special thanks to Cari Cole and Judy Sleek. Our "official" W Bunch photographer, Bev Jones, sent me numerous pictures of our group. Jimmie Moomaw has been my writing mentor and gave me valuable advice all along the way. Thanks to each of you for your generous gift of time to help me get this manuscript ready.

And thanks to my dearest friends of over 60 years, affectionately dubbed The W Bunch. You have been my cheerleaders and encouragers, willing to trust me when I recommended unfamiliar locales, and loving me even when my suggestions were less than ideal. How lucky we were to find each other all those years ago! And we have another trip in the making....

About the Author

Donette Dunaway Lee was born in the Mississippi Delta and grew up in the small farming community of Hollandale. At the request of her mother's younger sister, Donette was named after Suzette and her new husband Don.

Finishing Hollandale High School in the mid-fifties, she graduated from Mississippi State College for Women (now Mississippi University for Women) with a degree in Sacred Music. After several years at home with her children, she entered the business world and retired from BellSouth Telecommunications Company in 1994.

Though she had an interest in art her entire life, her small school did not offer any art instruction. Finally retirement brought the opportunity to take art lessons. Also due to the pressures of working, it was only after retirement that she was able to plan for visits to other countries. The combination of these two loves has provided many years of pleasure.

Lee lives in a senior community in Hiram, Georgia. Her two daughters, Larraine and Marietta, and their families also live in Georgia.

She added, "While writing the book, one of my precious grandchildren asked if I talked about them in my book. I had to say 'No', but for Margaret's sake, I am including their picture."

Tristan *Margaret* *Avery* *Zach*
age 13 *age 9* *age 4* *age 11*

Made in the USA
Middletown, DE
06 November 2014